Passion's Fire

NLWEISER

AuthorHouse™ LLC
1663 Liberty Drive
Bloomington, IN 47403
www.authorhouse.com
Phone: 1-800-839-8640

Published by AuthorHouse 12/23/2013

ISBN: 978-1-4918-4048-1 (sc)
*   978-1-4918-4049-8 (e)*

Library of Congress Control Number: 2013923306

Any people depicted in stock imagery provided by Thinkstock are models,
and such images are being used for illustrative purposes only.
Certain stock imagery © Thinkstock.

This book is printed on acid-free paper.

author HOUSE®

Acknowledgments

I would like to thank poets Maya Angelou, Robert Frost, Pablo Naruda, Kahil Gibran, and T.S. Elliot for filling my mind with beautiful examples. I would also like to thank the Penn Women organization and the McKendree Writer's club for their patient ears and insightful suggestions. . In particular I would like to thank club members, Wanda Patterson, Hunter Dunn and Grace Welch who believed in me and insisted I keep on writing. Also there were online poetry clubs with members such as Poetatlarge, Midnight Eyes, Glenys Carr and Anne Dean who shared and shaped many of my writings and poems. My late husband, Charles Weiser, I must thank for being my cheering section and being the source for most of my poems. I would also like to thank my friend and soul- sister, Jean Lowry for proof reading my strange spellings. And last but not least I would like to thank my son, Mike Weiser for providing photographic illustrations for my written memories.

WORDS
Sept 25th 2012

I seek words. Words that have meaning
Words that embrace you; enfold you in lover's arms.
Let them pound with the insistent
Power of life's heart beat.
Let them be sounds shouted from a mountain top
That slide, echoing down the majestic mountain
Of long, hard earned experience.
Let them bounce bravely in the brain with
Hot truths, and snow cold purities.
Then let tempered meaning explode
Across the air waves of time.
Reaching valley's bottom let it
Tenderly touch a waiting soul's awareness.
Then, with a glow like quick silver, let such words
Shine, then endure, after one's final days.

PASSION'S FIRE

Dedicated with love to Charles Weiser

CONTENTS

Section One: Passion's Fire

Ambrosia of Life

Whenever it happens, love that is,
It sweetly happens for it tis'
Truly the most tossed and toasted
Shredded coconut treat of ever lovin' life.

Sometimes it occurs in hairy chatter...
Monkey like... swingin' and swearin'.
Sometimes it's   in sliding silk limbed silence.
Which and whatever way... then there is life..

I dream, in order to remember,
Your whispers of love, your bedroom eyes
Your satin hardness and its pulsing
Dance before my, oh so yearning sighs.

I tremble as the abyss opens
To your slamming heat and our
Ambrosia of life mixes, flows, and
Races toward a screaming rip-tide.

As you plunge down, oh so far down,
A high wind blows fanning the flame
Of hot desire which whips and licks
The animal deep within desire untamed.

With splash, jerk, and explosion I come
Back arched and screaming into sunshine.
Dream of love you are like ambrosia,
Sweet taste of love. The very the essence of life.

Belly Dance For Gypsy Fiddler

You touched me, my Gypsy lover,
And made shivers slide down my spine.
Little did I know how you'd stir me.
Thus stealing my love for all time.

Each word of your honey lipped murmurs
Was like jewels in a diamond cut room.
Their facets did blind and bind me
Until slavishly I begged to be thine.

Close your eyes, I begged gypsy fiddler
As you play on the strings of my heart.
For they lure, and mock and wantonly tease
All that is women and longs to please.

I undress like a drunken strip-teaser
Belly dance with tinkling bells
Nipples hard were caressed with abandon
And his playing demanded even more.

Shimmy, gyrate it demanded as
His fiddling around passion did soar.
Then he stopped and said, come lay in my arms
Let us feast on your pomegranate's amour.

Dark Mist

5/28/2007

You, my dark mist of damp dreams
Whisper sweet longings to my surf.
The wash of vermilion passion
Brings hope to my death gray soul.

I awaken and love's soaring is erased
Like beach sand around a driftwood frame.
The distant caw of a raven reminds me
That what once was is never more.

Dragon Lust
9/22/2000

Seeking, he wanders in dragon lust
Flaming all souls caught with in path's need.
In lust feeding madness I quiver,
As I gaze into his beady eyed greed.

Frozen to the spot by his magnificence,
He is, after all, the jewel of the world.
On the open field I prostrate myself, and plead
For taking, as his mind link within me swirls.

His answering thunder rumbles, shaking the earth.
And his moan tears the curtain of love's soul.
One by one I pound in the tethering pegs
And announce to the world he is mine alone.

A burnished gold pillar bridges lip moistening desire.
Huge golden globes swing and tease their potency.
Then suddenly he takes me with his diamond hard lance,
And skewers hot pleasure upon its great length.

Deep wells of dewed honey spew forth.
Coating all with sweet nectar of love.
While I screech with orgasmic abandon he
Trumpets, "Chosen one." And we soar forever free.

Dream Catcher
@2007

You, my feather, my tickling tease
Intricate web 'round spread desire
Caress dreamless nights wild longing.
As I, like Dream Catcher, hang…,
Leather bound, Above taunt cradle of need.

Your spider thin words of avowed love
Light creeping, long-legged in
Midnight darkness catch, hold
With intricate web weavings
Screaming nightmare at bay.

Through the web into the night
I desperately soar as you build me,
Rock me, fill my moon's pulling center
Until, like lightning charged I
Blast from need to a blinding star.

Dream Caught Time
@ 20001

In the calligraphy of dream caught time
I behold the radiance of our love.
Indelibly inked, on rice paper fine,
It slashes, like a Japanese wood block
Its bold exquisite hues across my heart.

Wind chimes outside my bedroom window
Delicately whisper sweet nothings in my ear.
Wild gypsy music floods my soul.
At twilight, framed by lacy tree limbs
I dream the pull of man's desires.

Rocked in the cradle of the crescent moon
I moan tender sighs then open reluctant eyes.
Harsh time shifts and that which was is not.
How quickly dreams vanishes. Oh God, I beg,
Please give me back my dream caught time.

Ode To My Love

7/12/2000

I open sweet lips of love.
The long thin finger of time
Swirls, coats and dips deep into
My cup of offering nectar.

You are the mind's seashore
Of hot melting grains of sand .
Your potency fills flared nostrils.
Desire grips my waiting hand.

You have the salty taste of iron.
I am awash in the very sea of you.
When I am with you all stands still.
Your wave undertows my solid ground.

Then I go swirling, screaming down.
Swiftly down into a waiting vortex
Of orgasmic pleasure so profound.
You, my love, are my ebb and tide.

Midnight Eyes

Two strangers pass filled with things unsaid.

One lovesick, heart starved, and empty.

She was lonely, so piteously lonely.

His marrow sucked bones long dead.

At midnight's eye his purring words

Fling her soul toward his hypnotic flame.

"Let me take you, my rosebud, flushed and glowing

Deep into the corners of your lust filled mind."

"Enter," beseech his bedroom eyes.

"Feel passion's rutting grunts and grind.

Swim like life's first amoebae toward an exploding riptide."

Suddenly screaming passion fills both their entwined minds.

"I shall call you my sweet Jasmine,"

You could almost hear his heartfelt sigh.

"Essence of pure joy, you've raised this Lazarus.

From despair you have helped me climb."

Wrapped in love's touch her heart broke asunder

When with abrupt click he said, Goodbye.

He had filled her lonely, love starved midnight.

But once again she was alone in the night.

Oiled

7/12/2000

Heated beads of oil
Lavishly drips from
Elongated fingers poised tips.

Sun worshipping flesh
Moans desire as cupped hands
Swirl twin peaked   intensity.

Flesh begs with soft sighs
For kneading strong hands
sensual, smooth stroking.

Out Of Hell's Darkness

2007

Within Hell's hot darkness are post tied limbs.
Hard eyes mock and view stark naked spread sin
Tongue of fear soon licks sweat slick skin
Room's cold silence mocks need so grim.

Come, my eyes beg in need's darkness,
Tame the hell of my life made grim.
Life bend my will to pliant taking
Bring me forth to a sub's hot rim.

A mist of sea green ocean
Washes over and above.
With screaming lips I fly and soar.
Does time exist without man's love?

Passion's Flower

7/12/2000

Misting
invisible
dew
floats
skin
of pink lipped
longing. Potent seed swelling
with need thrusts self on passion's
groaning. Delving deep into lava
caves flowering passions
flowing.

Shattered Mirror

8/23/2000

The shine of your eyes, like a shattered mirror,
Reflects the wantonness of my slivered soul.
Mocking all sense of modesty I
Lie naked and whorishly bold.

The hyena laugh of glutinous need
Shatters hot night's smothering greed.
Goading stroke after lust filled stroke
With screeching, demonic screams.

Deep within the broken crystal of my heart
Tinkles down, down endlessly   down
To shred the pit of my once pure soul.
For I know, tearfully , love was never known.

Whiff

7/12/2000

So sweet your scented presence.
Can you whiff my scent of desire?
Like herbs of thyme, mint and basil
You're the root in my earth of fire.

Life Is but a precious moment
Moth fluttering before eternal time.
Shall I pluck the leaves before me
And steep in pleasure's climb.

You may mint my precious tulips
Until one by one I collapse inside.
Then root of sin I beg enter in
For too soon the cold earth dies.

Section Two: Water's Edge

Dewdrop

7/12/2000

Dewdrop reflects
Thine Image as it
Quivers before
Tongues touch.
Silver blue it quivers,
One drop, then two…
Waiting, waiting
In the pink washed room.
Purple, rose tipped
Hunger lies
Just beyond
Times reach.
Splashing down…
With silent sound,
From midnight's
Black,
black ink.

Glacier Slide

5/27/2007

At glacier I spy death cold pleasure,
And make a slow ice picked ascent.
As hot tongue licks frozen tundra I
Rope grip with courage summit's attempt.

Back packed survival, like melted ice,
Slides down the throat of star studded night.
Melting surface glistens it's need as
O'er snow-bridge I crawl tentatively.

Gripping clamps steal breathe from lungs as
Hanging by ropes o'er the edge I plunge.
My screams the mountain echoes around.
As I straddle the summit of hard pleasure found. .

Hope Surrendered
5/28 2007

Hope surrenders in salt rubbed silence.
Pain cries inside as you enslave my longing.

On soul's core you drip dream after dream
Mercilessly pounding its chaotic lust:
Lust for life,   lust for love, lust for belonging.

Eye's cold and uncaring suck hope's shine.
Freezing hope forever in this black hole of time.

Jazz Town Rain

2001

Oil slick puddles shimmer their rainbows tonight
As shoulder padded jackets slip slide from sight.
"Danger slick pavement," warns taxi cab beams.
As wipers tap dance like a click clacking team.

A strip dancing drum roll vibrates the air as
Deluging rain clouds flash flood the home crowd.
The wheels whine a sing song called, "Blue Berry Hill."
Zig -zagging light seems to shutter stop tired souls.

Jazz town is caught now in a dream like state.
Where pictures peep out and ghost dance past dates.
Grim Reaper approaches and waves you near, as
Time's ticking stop-watch clangs loud in the ear.

Iridescent Bubbles
@5/28/2007

In iridescent bubble blown from thin wire wand
Floats my secret self, the child that is me.
Eyes wide with wonder, be-spelled by your smile,
I clap my pure joy,   and it swirls, floats
Over gray beards,
Over heart's aching,
Over rainbow-fine times.

You chase thin walled beauty, floating so high. .
But cavalier you, ignoring the danger,
Seeing my trust,   kiss my brow.
I burst with a whispered sigh.

Now I am but a rainbow soap slither
That stings a dreamer's eyes.
Inconsolably I weep
Over lost childhood,
Over loves great pain,
Over iridescent bubbles.

Lady Lake's Courtship

1999

The water licked with lapping tongue
The lichen on rocks that halted
Tides run. For,   Lady   Lake's
Courtship has just begun.

Jewels for my lady love
Winked sun's bold eye
Casting sparkles of diamonds
That swished as he sighed.

The evening's deep purple
Wrapped moon's hopeful gaze.
Lady Lake just ignored him
To search breezy haze.

As Lady Lake combed her flowing
Grass hair strands of silver flowed
Through the air causing awe-struck
Moon-beam to long to caress her.

Dark Lady Lake just waved off
Their advances   For she loved
The wandering West Winds
Stirring, brisk dances.

Portals
12/20/1999

Come open the door of a book's many rooms
Where hinges squeak as you fend off the gloom.
I fumble to unlace my doe skin dress as
By the touch of the words you caress my breast.

Like a lion in the night you enter in
And lick my thighs as the love dance begins.
Then suddenly words shift with a bawdy laugh
And   glass beads tinkle from a brothel's past.

A strange portal appears   from a Grecian past
That arches and bucks then holds   stead-fast.
I crawl through ice doors, descend into caves.
I pulse in the First Lake and brave the new day.

I touch the future and history's rim.
I skim the surface and deep within.
With friend and teacher on paper so thin
Word portals open the mind that bends..

Pool Of Dreams

2001

Enclosed in palm fronds lies pool of dreams
Amidst drifted sand it shimmers mirage greens.

Parch lipped nomad, withered by time,
Quenches dry hope as thirst does climb.

Skip-jacking pebbles cause ripples to swirl,
As pink, blue bubbles cause fairy's to   twirl.

Happiness rims the slip sliding brink
Please time freeze before dream sinks.

Sea Mist

1999

Polished time o'er time again
In ocean's deep mysterious span
Silently whispers pearl to man
Iridescent in my hard lipped clam
I grow in eternal eloquence.

Pure white gull swims azure sky.
Then feathered and waiting bobs ocean tide.
Like misty ghosts they arrive
To float so proud and eloquently

Silently I look at all life's views.
Each day, each hour unfolds its hues.
I see each person born anew
So each second are you too.
And oh, it is so eloquent.

River Currents
7/17/2000

In my women's depth flows many currents.
One's a raging river, crashing against the rock of time.
Heedless of life's roaring waterfalls it
Plummets to the rush of the sucking sea.
The rush itself is sought after to be
Tasted like a fine wine and stir the quiet.

One current run's shyly, wrapped in a morning mist.
Its surface is mirror still, reflecting, floating lazily in the sun.
Dreamy eyed it drifts in the breeze seeking quiet ponds
With lily pads in places where frogs croak and cicadas rub legs.
As moonbeams lantern the current it contemplates the whys.
Always listening,   it laps its waves on the shore of life.

One current drifts in silted mud and dirty fish guts.
It drags sluggishly through swamp fed bottoms.
Like a mud cat, it feeds on discarded   garbage.
Fat and goggle-eyed it views the uselessness of life.
Growing green with age it stinks of lost hopes
And grows purposeless with lack of sight.

One current is full of life. Diamond studded and wave dancing
It dares the willow tips tease and the rapid's passionate longings.
It courses through many channels. Some are bedrock deep and
Pierce the heart with poignant memories. Memories of fish egg beds,
Minnows well fed, and a mother's delight flood times river.

Sometimes, as I slowly meander and fog drift,
I see driftwood dreams all sunken in sand. And in
Mind's eye I fly with dragonfly wings to beautiful heights.
One day soon I shall chart my course toward the sea
As I float the ebb and ride the tide, baptized by life.

Rollin' The Jazz Town Rain
2007

As motor oil droplets seek puddles of quiet
Their purples form rainbows in Jazz Town tonight.
Slick pavement, there's danger eyes transit's hot beams.
As rain blankets blues wail of whining wheel screams.

The   flim-flaming raindrops softly tap dance the road.
Then drum rolling raincloud slam dunks a full load.
On corner sits hangout called Blueberry Hill
Where Scott Joplin ragtime is often the bill.

The bus stops to idle and horns take their licks
When patrons of Jazz Town don't bee-bop by quick.
The driver rives motor when passengers roar
"The levee has Dixieland! Put metal to floor"

Twilight Of The World
2007

In the twilight of the world
Man and women greet love's shine. .
Entwined together like two lovers
They gaze upon sweet heavens climb.

The sunset whispers seductively
Reflecting blushed crimsons and delicate pinks.
The clouds are trimmed with golden halos
As they float before love's door.

Ocean's of deep splash their longing
Lapping against hot lava shores.
Gentle waves caress earth's turning
As heaven opens and passions soar.

Like sands of time forever shifting
Love does linger through the night.
Mockingbirds sing that dreams are ending.
As indigo seas reflect starlight.

Section Three: Good Earth

Bodacious
7/12/2000 (High School memory)

I was bodacious, oh yes,
The pain of genetic whim.
"Here comes Robin Redbreast,"
Sneered boys with monkey limbs.

They punched each others shoulders,
Then drooled like dirty old men
At girls that walked the gauntlet
With blushes and embarrassed grins.

X-ray eyes fondled bodaciousness .
Perked nipples pushed sweater's skin.
Hormones raced with unbidden vileness
To be greeted by crotch swollen jeans.

My mind screamed like a banshee.
I was filled with boy banging dreams.
But I scurried past, with eyes downcast,
Before they could whiff Aphrodite's den.

Dream Teacher

1999

Hear the doors of dreamer's rooms
Where tanned hides flap or hinges squeak,
Or glass beads tinkle brothel tunes.

See the portals from Grecian past
That arch and buck then stand fast.
Where Socrates orates at the Acropolis.

Crawl through ice tunnels, dwell   in bat caves
Live in a whale or pulse in First Lake.
Touch the stars and history's rim.

Caress silk surfaces or deep within.
Concludes   my teacher, paper thin whose
Ink stained words can so mind bend.

Dust Brown Days

1965

The paddle-wheel of a threshing machine
Floats through an ocean of grain.

And in its wake a swath is cut
That perfumes the goldenrod day.

The sweet hay smell of country air
Fans memories of dust-brown days.

Days when the young shout "Double dog dares"
Then swing from the loft In wild "Tarzan" play.

Those childhood days of simple fun,
Race swifter than swallows in flight.

My dust-brown days are too far a run
For my hair has turned quite gray.

But I'll run the sun, when memory comes,
With the smell of fresh mown hay.

Fields Of Harm

2001

Out of body I ride the star-studded sky
In a dream of great winds and tide.
I glide between, two galaxy's gleams
As I star chase eternal quite .
Clinging in terror to Draco's head
I am pierced by his star- studded hide.

Looking space down it spins me to ground
To a field that's in harm's way. Where
Dali drawn thistles swish nettle crystals that
Tinkle like bourbon on ice. Their evil intent
Throws crystals through soft bodies in flight.

Why, oh war, must you chase me in horror
Even in fleeing solace of dreams.
I silently scream at fear feed scene.
That shatters repose of quite night.

Winked am I to another dream's clime
And yet another dread field of harm.
Where great coils creak, like memory deep
From stems spun from rusty bed springs.
Their cushion round heads entice with silk thread
And give promise of passion's delight.

They seductively sway at a sailor to stay
And sow wild oats while on shore leave.
Then thin needle of time bursts death's
Fungi, and scuds fill airways. Spraying nerve gas,
Blood and ash, that chokes young life away.

"To late," I cry. The world now dies and
Is covered with choking gray.
For horned Is the head that jabs it's dread
And feeds on all paralyzed life.

In worlds far away another field sways
As Zebra plants bray, "To Arms!"
They form up and march as if on a lark,
And charge through harm's field to prey.
With gas masks on, like rogue
Elephants they swarm. and trample life away.

In the corner of dread dream, in
Crevice unseen, sways a green the
Color of life. Humming hope to
Despair the clover clutches where
Trodden barren, the granite field's lie.

In a world much wronged vibrations of
Song, turn granite path to soft rich loam.
Where fields of green do freely cling
And man plants deep love of home.

Cicadas

2000

In hot breath of night drones the ancient message
Of leg rubbing cicadas discordant sighs.
Piercing and swelling with rapture is their mating.
As they swish soft shadow secrets to listening whys.
Flying and fluttering they blink tiny shutters in the restless quiet.

It's a mysterious window to a miniature world where
Thin legs crawl twig logs and hypnotize mind's sight.
It's an invasion of thousands upon thousands of insects
As sheer curtain clouds draw across moon's one eyed light.
Reflecting and refracting how small all are in God's grand night.

Garden Of Erotic Love
7/12/2000

I stand in love's garden,
Erotic garden of love,
Breathing, tasting, touching
The power of kisses hug.

Lips of pleasure stir zephyr
Breeze sending hummingbird
Kisses o'er nipples hot need. As
Lusts bright flash brings me to knee.

Languid eyes widen as passion soars.
Nostrils flare wide and heart gives a roar.
Rabbit scared I search the tall grass
For a cave secure to hide me fast.

Be not afraid. Let us feast in the sun.
Jeweled words are my bind and hold my run.
Blindfolded by lust I grab for his thrust.
To be torn by his silence and leave taking rush.

Now I can see he was but snake in the grass.
Slithering and sliming o'er feelings so fast.
Grabbed from behind I saw not his burning.
Pleasure so shallow is not worth soil's turning.

Gran's Amber Years

1961

Small cedar box with blemishing knots
Secures Gran's amber years.
Its mellow top has spider cracks;
(A wrinkled face from veil of tears.)

Wood corners lock, four square secure,
Like a love meshed family.
Dainty is latch of tarnished brass
To be lifted reverently.

My grandchild eyes, now aged and wise,
Behold her bejeweled youth.
In mind's eye a tale is spun
From fragmented bits of truth.

A snake of copper slithers by
On a pin with pearl drop leaf.
It's hypnotic eyes, and sibilant sighs:
Was a gift from a slick-haired thief.

Vague memory speaks of tale once told
Of a boat called the River Queen.
Whose gambler stole child's gift of love
Then… fled to New Orleans.

Long kept was gift once given Gran
Then locked in jewelry box.
I wonder how oft she held it close.
And dreamed of love's lost hope?

So Bleeds My Soul

20001

I'm a candy wrapper discarded.
My sweet, sticky fullness sucked dry.
"Tis on dirty street stomps cruel lover's feet.
Can you hear my shattered cry?

Gone are times tender moments.
Gone is a gentle goodbye.
Passion fades within the ghost of a day.
So bleeds this soul felt lie.

Peace Lily
2000

You were given to me on this,
The dreariest of life's days.
I, a woman   no longer loved,
Ashen of soul and hips without sway.

Dull eyes entered greenery
Sucking them to gray.
Yet, you leafed proudly,
Defiantly, and wouldn't go away.

Flower's bent hood of praying grace
Made pain pulse the air and slap the face.
Begging Angel of Mercy to wrap death around
I traveled your roots to tombs sacred ground.

Its neck stretched tall and impossibly thin
Like the Angel of Death that you'd welcomed in.
Your sweet touch of marble on wax embalmed skin
In Peace Lily's arms I beheld once again.

The Mistletoe

1992

In midwinter's creaking cold
On the isle of Celts of old,
Grows an ancient, leafless grove
Of sacred bark-bound druid souls.

Proud and tall stands one such oak
A beacon to the ancient folk
To keep true all holy seen
With mistletoe of fertile green.

The firm berries form a crown,
And from the mistletoe hang down,
Like budding breasts of maidens fair,
They press the cloth of mystic air.

Enters grove on Christmas Eve,
Filled with youthful purity,
A knightly lad, with curly tresses,
Longing   for his love's caresses.

The mistletoe's ancient power
Tugs his memory while in bower.
With merry twinkle in his eye,
He climbs from mist to treasure high.

Like druid priest of long ago
He hurries home with mistletoe.
O'er his door he hangs the leaves:
Oval,   smooth like lips that tease.

Looking up true love is caught,
And pays, as is traditions lot,
With magic mystic kiss of love
The lips of eager lad above.

Voytak, The Goatman
1987

Shunning the world of warring man,
Voytak stood on sun faded land.
Tintype still, with mustard gassed lungs,
He struggled to breathe in the moist, hot sun.

In muddled head he dreamed away and
Pulled on his long, white beard as he swayed.
He tried to remember sweet days before
When there was peace, and friends died no more.

Instead, to his mind came rivers of blood
Where youth had been but fodder for war
From battle and carnage at French Verdun
He could still hear the booming big guns.

The bleat of the goats were his tears,
For his eyes were sealed with unbearable pain.
Lost peace was sought as he paced the woods
Trying to escape mind's winter rain.

Finality

@1997

It is done. All that ever was. All one ever willed.
The thing now named. FINALITY…The
Stopping a start. The beginning
Ever ending. Until life's

Final end. Which Is the

Beginning of the

Beginning or…..

The beginning

Of the

End.

Section Four: Breath of Air

A Clothes'pin Review

1999

Washday pine pigeons , chorus line straight,
Precariously perch on the clothesline's   white face.
Their monkish round knob-heads bob rigid how-doos
At the wispy shear panties that strip-tease the view.

A mother's stiff scrub hands ruff red from hard work
Tote soggy diapers that announce a new birth.
Grip hard, my forked pigeons. Stay on the line.
For so hangs the fate of the young and divine.

Among Silver Crystals Of Snow
by Nancy Weiser 1987

```
 *       *       *       *       *       *       *
    *       *       *       *       *       *
       *       *       *       *       *
```

```
            < >
           (A-)
           mong
          SiL-ver
         Crys-tals
        of heavenly
        @@@ @@@
       ****SNOW****
     @Children's eager@
     Faces do softly glow.
     @@@@@ @@@@@
    **Among silver crystals**
    ***of snow,*** (of snow).***
    @@@@@@   @@@@@@
   *With tones as clear as crystals
    Sung childishly loud, they pierce the
   Cold silence of homes gathered round. A-
   mong silver crystals of snow,** (of snow). *
    @@@@@ @@@@@   @@@@@@
   *Cold cheeks so apple rosy and tingling ice toes *
   Are welcomed all in by hearts once cold. Among silver
   Crystals of snow, *** (of snow).*** H O T marshmellow
   choc'late a steaming in pans 'twill WARM the cold children's
   @@@@@@    @@@@@@ @@@@@@ @@@@@@
   @ tiny gloved hands. **** Among silver crystals of snow. ****@
   ** (of snow), ** 'Twas a gift of song and a gift of LOVE upon the**
   *Eve of God's gift from above .** Among silver crystals of heavenly*
            (SNOW)
           ::::::::::::::
```

Beyond The Sunset

The day is ending beyond the sunset
Of pink pigs and dancing flamingos.
A crown of purple passion fingers
A lava pit of restless yearning.

A powerful, allusive image ghosts
Through the wind-devils of her mind
Then he whirls, twirls, dervishes away
Much too deep for memory to find.

She seeks distractions, entertainments,
Passionate couplings that pierce like
Hot ash through paper thin dreams
Then burst into consuming flame.

It is evening now. Turning earth quietly
Pulls midnight's peace o'er the velvet sky.
Sweet sleep brings the power of his passionate
Touch for all time… beyond the sunset.

Doe-Eyed Enigm
200

Sh ..be quiet, for one of life's
Secrets hugs the brisk morning.
It tiptoes out of a thicket
Of silent nature's seclusion.
Where a nest of lacy ferns
Surrounded by bramble bush thorns
Shields this doe-eyed enigma.

Sun dappled by leaves it quivers and seeks

One weeps at such beauty's intrusion.

A twig snaps glades peace then with

Rainbow shaped leaps it silently

Flees the barb of cruel hunters.

Phillyloo

1997

Like a wigwam tripod on a high rise square
My step skips different on the road to where.
Phillyloo, Phillyloo.

Like birds in the never that fly upside down
I heat with the beat of a jazz wail sound.
Phillyloo, Phillyloo.

Rose colored creams and burnished blacks
Rock fandangels on the straight red path.
Phillyloo, Phillyloo.

Life grows to finish. The end begins.
Soul bends backward to start again.
Oolyllihp, Oolyllihp, Oolyllihp.

Cobwebs

1997

When cobwebs cling to ancient
Bones and gray gravestones,
I'll dream a dream as rich as cream
Of that childhood that clings to me .

Where rainbows slide in sapphire skies
Reflected in my mind's eye
Is monkey me climbing a tree
In a past when this child ran free.

It's a tree as tall as a Mom or Dad
That shades a young girl or an intelligent lad.
As cobwebs cling and my memory dreams
I swing on the limbs a of solid oak past.

Shadow Of Dawn

1950

The shadow of dawn is a crawling thing,
Diaper wet, grubby hand and reaching.
In time's blink of eye morning arrives
Stretching it's shadow into childhood.

That shadow climbs trees, skinning its knees
And   runs   the sun with   great glee.
It grows in great bounds from the lessons found.
Then, with a yawn, it playfully moves on.

Then stretches its shadow to noon time.
The peak of its power now touches
And towers   oe'r its chosen life purpose.
Too soon dusk arrives shrinking its size.

Bat size it beats toward seclusion.
Then with misty eyes the shadow
Cries for coming night soon swallows
The shadow of life's grand illusions.

Star Burst

1997

Ancient blue radiance's death throe
Throbs with exploding birthing pain.
In desperation it bursts and flings
Itself into swaddling voids domain.

The micro dust huddles and gathers
Then bravely swirls in dance of life.
Embryo organism and hydrogen cloud
Touch then embrace like man and wife.

Magnetic pull quickly melds them to one
And desire drives new star to flash into light.
As life is to death and death is to life
From hydrogen cloud to stellar ash white.

How wonderful that carbon based us
So many light years away may
View the glow of a red dwarf star
And know that darkness holds no sway.

Sunset Brunches
5/28/2007

I seek smooth pebbles today.
Whiffs of freshly brewed coffee,
Stroking of purring cat fur,
Necked stretching on smooth silk sheets.

Love's flitting shapes smile memory's eyes
Then, like swallows at dusk, they fly away.
Leaving silver vapor trails on warm sheets
Like spent bullets from lost love's pain.

Stark branches of ink lace the blue sky.
Home for nesting birds and birds of prey.
Sensing all life's yearning today I
Feel tree's hard trunk and boiling sap rise.

With wild clinging musk of earth in air
The breeze makes branches flay love's sky.
Sap of woman, trunk of man: such is life.
In the tree is the very nature of time.

Even in Sunset's blushing shades.
Even as day fades slowly away.
The circle of life twirls and bows
Then spins back again each day.

Tap Dance Kid

2000

Do a rhythm tap to make a flash.
Parrididdle, parrididdle, slide and glide.
Rip slide, ebb tide, pucker petals wide.
Shuffle hop, hip hop, Shirley Temple dive.

Let booty swing o'er your pinnacles' gleam
As you break to the left with a pelvic swing.
Then it's huckle buckle rock
With a boogie woogie cock.

"Shake it baby," moans a greasy haired Gene.
As I ass slap clickity clack, spank and swing.
Motown flashes a dancer's dream as
Lights flash, crowds pack to see me cream.

Dusting the boards till the cows come home
I boom boom bump and grind to make them groan.
I ball his jack with a graceful attack.
As I snare drum tap a wicked slap whack.

Toys In The Attic

1997

Like toys in attic are tossed dreams.
As time hour glasses away
Discarded hopes rock back and forth
On cracked hobby horse stiff legs.

Fragile, mold smelling pages of
Used books are leaves that turn today.
Needed are brooms to clean attic's room
And new toys with which to play.

Dust piled and cobwebbed are torn
Thoughts in corners of worn mind.
I must hurry and paint bright scenes
For sunlight, to soon must fade.

On stilted legs the causeway flees
The wet sand where beach bums wade.
So to, shall I go adventuring some day
Way beyond where fisher folk sing and play.

Fresh cut flowers perfume dusty attic
And brighten what's left of dawning days.
Broken dreams in attic I'll leave to the jade.
For the wild child in me still longs to play.

Wild Beastie Orchestra

1999

In the Grand concert hall
Wild Beastie Orchestra's
Discordant tune-ups   grate the ear
And run, oh so merrily amuck.

Bleating goat brasses
Back of stage wah wah's
Nag the doddlin' clarinets,
And quacking oboe ducks.

A formal white tied penguin
Waddles quickly up stage
Hushing monkey fiddlers
Right out of Jungle Book.

Pecking on his music stand,
The notes look like a bird seed fan,
He flaps his wings and nods his head
And makes the music soar.

They play so grand the angels cry.
It ends and weeping willows sigh.
Concert goers stomp for more
Then give a Lion King's roar.

The Windmill

1999

In the mist of fading time
When life no longer shines,
Unchallenged windmills click and
Sneer then spin stiff limbs of pine.

Their challenge whirrs and stirs the
Air and fans old warrior's flame.
Though weak I seek to circle the dare
Like a moth toward death's   game.

I shake my fist, defiantly,
At the windmills in my mind
Then pull my chin with chagrin
And try to remember why.

Printed in the United States
By Bookmasters